# BIRDS, ROOTS, WEEDS, AND THE GOOD GROUND

## THE PARABLE OF THE SOWER

## Dr. John F. Avanzini

# The Parable of the Sower

The Parable of the Sower is a very familiar one which anyone who has studied the Word of God will quickly recognize. It is a rather simple illustration of a very complex spiritual truth.

The importance of this subject becomes evident when we realize just how complex the environment of any living thing is.

My dictionary defines environment as "all of the surrounding conditions and influences that affect the development of a living thing". It is obvious that a person's character is influenced by his environment. Differences in environment often account for irregularities in plants of the same species. Given the proper environment, as opposed to a hostile environment, one plant will thrive while another will wither. The Parable of the Sower — the story that Jesus told in the fourth chapter of the Gospel of Mark, is an illustration of the effect spiritual environment has on a "good seed's" growth and fruitfulness.

Mark 4: 1-20

# Chapter 1

# Environment Is the Key to Growth

When we look around us today, we can see that there is a great deal of concern about our environment. Those in the construction industry, as well as those seeking to buy new homes, are keenly aware of environmental problems. Probably a third of the cost of a new home is related to environmental protection. Environmental conditions have become a very important consideration in selecting a home.

In the Parable of the Sower, we read about the seed and are told that the seed is the Word of God. Normally, seeds are planted in dirt. The Bible tells us that Adam was "The Dirt Man" and that he was formed from the dust of the earth. Here God brings the gospel to Adam in the form of seed. The very word "seed" is a translation of the Greek word "spora", which means "sperm". So we see that the "sperm" of God is spread about the human race. When it falls on the ground of our heart, if the **environment** is good, the seed will grow.

When we begin to closely examine what we read in the Parable of the Sower, we become aware that the parable is simply telling us about different environmental problems and how each affects the fruitfulness of plants. We now realize just how much environment has to do with the growth of seed.

The parable tells us about one environmental problem known as birds. Farmers are often troubled with birds. The use of scarecrows and different types of noise-making devices in their fields help to prevent birds from eating the seed. Birds are often considered **devastating** to the farmer!

## THE HOSTILE ENVIRONMENT

A healthy environment is the controlling factor in the kind of growth a plant will have and in the production and quality of its fruit.

There are various environmental factors that influence a plant's growth and production of fruit. If you plant a tree in a hostile environment, it will quickly wither and die. The cause could be too much or too little sunlight, food or water. In the bathroom at home, I have a fern hanging over the bathtub. It looks very attractive there, but it exists in a hostile environment. Because it lacks something vital to growth, it is not doing well there.

## ROOTS ARE ALSO
## SUBJECT TO ENVIRONMENT

There is a little worm known as the cutworm who lives underground. It is a part of the environment. When it gets into your fields it goes almost unnoticed, but suddenly the plants just fall over. Actually, cutworms move around underneath the ground, and when they reach a root, they cut it. They don't seem to eat it all — just a section of it, but they thoroughly destroy the crops. The cutworm adversely affects the ability of the roots to supply the plant with the nourishment it needs to survive.

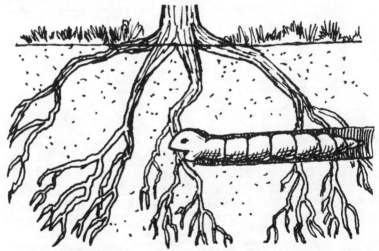

## WEEDS ARE PART OF
## THE HOSTILE ENVIRONMENT

There are many destructive weeds. When you have weeds in your garden you have a very poor garden. When my family lived in St. Petersburg, Florida, we, as real estate developers, would buy grapefruit and orange orchards and turn them into subdivisions for housing. The fruit trees were weed infested and would yield small, skimpy, sour, fruit. Waist high weeds and vines grew all over those trees and they looked terrible! There is nothing more disorderly than an orchard that has been taken over by weeds.

The people who moved into the newly built homes cut down the weeds and the vines. The remaining fruit grew strong again. My wife and I often ate the fruit from those trees for our breakfast. Those same orchards that had been so run down and weed inundated now produced beautiful fruit. With the hostile environment of weeds gone, the trees again became fruitful.

# Chapter 2

# Birds, Roots, Weeds and the Good Ground

The parable of the sower tells us about good seed that fell on good ground, and began to bring forth some thirty, some sixty, and some a hundred fold.

Turning to Mark 4:3, we read: *"Behold, there went our a sower to sow: And it came to pass, as he sowed, some fell by the way side, and the fowls of the air came and devoured it up. And some fell on stony ground, where it had not much earth; and immediately it sprang up, because it had no depth of earth:*

*But when the sun was up, it was scorched; and because it had no root, it withered away. And some fell among thorns, and the thorns grew up and choked it, and it yielded no fruit. And other fell on good ground, and did yield fruit that sprang up and increased; and brought forth, some thirty, and some sixty, and some a hundred fold."*

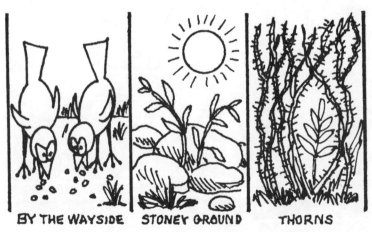

BY THE WAYSIDE    STONEY GROUND    THORNS

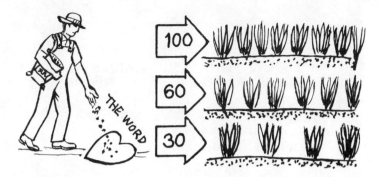

If you look further to the 14th verse, Jesus explains what the seed in the parable meant. He said, *The sower soweth the word.* We find that the seed of this parable is the Word of God.

*And these are they by the way side, where the word is sown; but when they have heard, Satan cometh immediately, and taketh away the word that is sown in their hearts.* This part of the parable I refer to as the action of "birds" on the good seed that is sown.

*And these are they likewise which are sown on stony ground; who, when they have heard the word, immediately receive it with gladness; And have no root in themselves, and so endure but for a time afterward, when affliction or persecution ariseth for the word's sake, immediately they are offended.* This part of the parable I refer to as the weakness of a poor root system.

*And these are they which are sown among thorns; such as hear the word, And the care of this world, and the deceitfulness of riches, and the lusts of other things entering in, choke the word, and it becometh unfruitful.* These are the unproductive seeds which I refer to as being destroyed by "weeds".

*And these are they which are sown on good ground; such as hear the word, and receive it, and bring forth fruit, some thirty fold, some sixty and some a hundred.* I interpret the term "good ground" as meaning an orderly, controlled environment conducive to the growth and multiplication of the "seed".

## "BIRDS"

The first truth we grasp as we do an environmental study of Mark 4:15, is that the environment which is first mentioned to us is where the seed devouring birds live.

Now as we follow this verse of scripture, we realize that Jesus used the plural — "birds". In His explanation to the disciples, Jesus said that Satan doesn't come to each and every individual on the planet every time he deals with them. We know that he uses principalities, powers, and wicked spirits as well as armies of demons to work for and with him.

It is true that the devil is called 'The Thief'. Think with me a moment. What does a thief do? He steals! After being robbed, you are impoverished!

Many times we find that when people are impoverished by Satan they turn around to the very one who is the giver, our great God, and they say, "Lord, why have you done this to me?"

They ignorantly say, "Well, I guess God wants me to be poor, I guess God wants me to have bad health, — or I guess God just wants me to do without."

The Bible doesn't teach that God wants you to do without. On the contrary, he wants you to have many wonderful things! Remember, child of God, the devil

is the one who has come to steal from you, and to take things away from you. Remember what we read in the second chapter of the Book of Revelation, "Hold fast that which thou hast".

Living on Planet Earth is much like being out on tour in a foreign country. As you come near the market place, your guide will turn to you and say, "Hold on to your pocketbook. There are pickpockets in this market." As a result, you go through the market with your hand in your pocket so that your pocketbook won't be taken.

Dear friend, while you're walking around on Planet Earth, hold fast to your pocketbook because the devil is trying to steal everything that God wants you to have. We come to find that this thievery — these Satanic 'birds' — are totally and absolutely against you and the things of God. Seeking to rob you, they will stop at nothing to take what is yours. They must be controlled.

## 'BIRDS' COME IN MANY FORMS

Have you ever noticed that when you try to witness to someone about Jesus, something often happens. You begin by saying, "I'd like to tell you..." Suddenly their phone rings.

They answer, "Oh! Uncle George! You're coming to visit us. You haven't come here in years." Then they

turn to you and say, "You will have to excuse me, because Uncle George is coming. I really want to hear what you have to say, but it will have to be some other time." That's the devil sending those 'birds' to steal the Word of God.

Now, we know that the Bible talks about a shaking in the last days. I maintain that one of the things the shaking will do is to shake those 'birds' out of our trees! You must get this firmly in your mind — that when you go into the farming business of God, planting the good seed of God, you need to see to it that the 'birds' are kept away from that good seed.

## WHEN YOU SEE THE BIRDS, DON'T SHOW THEM THE SEED

I have had people ask me after a brief encounter with a lost person, "Why didn't you witness to that

man or to that woman? How come you didn't tell them about Jesus?"

Dear friend, realize that it isn't always conducive to tell a person about Jesus. Sometimes it is better to be kind to that person, and let him see Christ in you.

Let me explain further. I've watched people going up in an elevator. A rider will push the button for the third floor. So up we go — floor one, floor two, floor three. A Christian will start witnessing to this person who is only going to the third floor! That is not the time for a long, drawn-out testimony. You may have a 'bird' sitting on the third floor waiting to steal the seed. Instead, leave a tract with him and always leave a smile with him. You could tell him how much God really loves him.

You don't have to have a closing every time you witness. There are times when you should just 'water' some. The seed may already have been planted and be hiding under the soil — awaiting some water so it can grow! Remember — one plants, one waters, **God gives the increase.**

Salesmen know that you can't close every deal, every time. Sometimes you have to wait for a better day. There may be a 'bird' sitting there trying to sell another product, and each time you bring up something about your product — he brings up an objection. The thing to do is wait until the opposition is removed. Then get back to your prospect and bring him to Christ without the threat of the 'birds' stealing the seed. You **must** watch for 'birds', because 'birds' present a hostile environment to growth.

## OPEN YOUR SPIRITUAL EYES

Simply open your spiritual eyes and you will see 'birds' sitting or flying all about the room. These 'birds' have come to steal! Think of it, spiritural 'buzzards' are looking you over right now, as you read!

Please look at Matthew :13. This will amaze you! Do you want to know where the 'birds' stay? Starting Matthew 13:31, the Bible tells of another parable Jesus put forth unto them.

*The kingdom of heaven is like to a grain of mustard seed, which a man took and sowed in his field. Which indeed is the least of all seeds: but when it is grown, it is the greatest among herbs, and becometh a tree, so that the birds of the air come and lodge in the branches thereof.*

Do you want to know where the 'birds' are hanging around? The 'birds' are in the tree of the king-

dom. They are hanging around our ministries to steal the seed when we sow it. A wise farmer will see to it that the 'birds' are under control in the place where he is sowing.

Don't think that just because you go to church there will be no 'birds' there. I've heard some people say, "Evil spirits at the church? Never!" Mark my words, the 'birds' hang around **in the tree of the kingdom!** I am convinced that there are not nearly as many spirits down at the neighborhood bar as there are around the church! Remember — 'birds' **steal** the Word of God when it's planted in the hearts of the people.

# Chapter 3

# The Root System

Not only do we have to take care of the 'birds' that are up in the air, but we have to be very careful about the root system under the ground. There must be a proper environment for the root system. Romans 11:18 says that the root bears the tree, not that the tree bears the root. When you see a tree, it is standing there because of the root system.

As with every building that is going to be built, before you can design the 20th floor, you must design a twenty floor foundation under it. There has to be a 'root' system under the building to support those twenty floors. There cannot be vital, on going, fruitful life without a good root system.

What does Jesus say? He says that you wash the outside of the cup and leave the inside dirty! It is painfully obvious that the greater part of Christianity is lived for people to see from the outside rather than for what is going on, on the **inside.**

The average Christian today could not stand an inspection of what is going on behind closed doors. He could not stand to have his root systems looked at because most Christians have a root system that is rotten, full of sickness, completely decayed and decrepit. We have become used to polishing only the **outside** of the cup.

Wake up, Christian! You can't build any kind of a quality Christian life that has a rotten and decaying root system under it! If your Christianity won't stand up behind closed doors, you had better understand that it won't stand up behind the closed doors of the Judgement of God.

An essential part of the environment of a good Christian life is a sound and solid root system. It's the

# CHRISTIAN ROOT SYSTEM

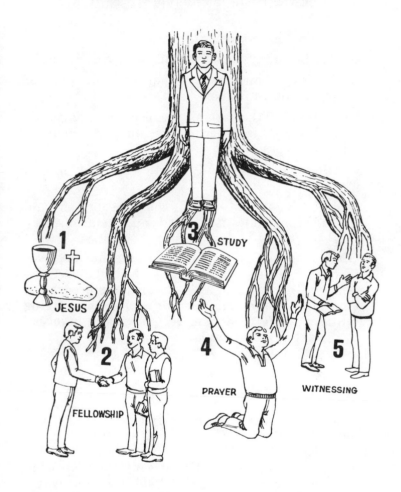

root system that feeds the tree. What does our parable say? It says that there was not root under some of the bushes. When they sprang forth, they sprang forth with nothing more than leaves and produced no fruit.

**Listed here are some basic building exercises for Christians.**

1. Learning the basic foundation truths from God's word.

   A. The blood atonement.

   B. The fact that Christ is risen and will return.

   C. The overcoming power that is in the name of Jesus and in prayer.

2. Not forsaking the assembling of yourself with the Church of God in order to worship and fellowship with believers.

3. Continuous Bible study, both personal and in groups.

4. Building your faith with constant prayer and fellowship with Jesus as 'Lord and Master' of every facet of your life.

5. Obedience to God's Word and personal involvement in fulfilling the directive of The Great Commission — to go into all the world and preach the Gospel to every living person — **become a living witness for Jesus and to get personally involved in the salvation of souls.**

## LEAFY TREES BEARING NO FRUIT?

Have you ever seen the leafy Christians? If you were to pack them in a rocket and shoot them to the moon, there is nothing in the Kingdom of God that would stop functioning because of their absence. There's not one little Sunday School child who would not be taught, nor one offering that wouldn't be taken. There's not one less person who would get the gospel. They do absolutely nothing but bear leaves. Many times those leaves are so pretty that shallow people will say, "Oh, if I could only be like them."

I want to tell you something about Jesus. **Jesus is not looking for shade!** He is looking for fruit! Bring

NEVER AGAIN
BEAR FRUIT

to remembrance what happened when Jesus met the fruitless fig tree that had only leaves.

When Jesus came and saw the tree with leaves only, He said, "Why are you covering the ground, you cursed bush? Never again will you bear fruit." And it withered and died.

Many say, "Preacher, you have to understand. I'm leafy!" But friend **God is not looking for shade.** God is looking for fruit! The truth is that many times some seemingly insignificant little saint in some Sunday School class — seeing about the matters of the Kingdom — taking care of the vineyard — is more valuable to God than some of the leafiest of saints.

## LEAFY PRIMA DONNAS

Often our churches are filled with prima donnas who move along in the leaf realm. How different is the appearance of a tree that is really bearing fruit! Once I noticed a small tree at a friend's house. You should

have seen it! That tree was so laden with fruit that it had sticks under its limbs to hold them up. It had hardly any leaves at all, but was heavy with fruit. Some of the limbs had even broken under the weight of the fruit it bore — but what a tree! It bore fruit — fruit — fruit! Praise God for those little trees that bear fruit instead of only leaves.

I have found this to be all too true: you can get anybody to be a prima donna. There's a **waiting list** to get to be a prima donna! But there's not a waiting list of people to clean the building. There's always a waiting list for people to sing 'Specials', but there doesn't seem to be a waiting list for joining the choir. There's always someone who wants the upper seat, but it's a real problem to get enough people to do the teaching in the Sunday school. You can always get people to sit at the tables, but it's a problem to get people to wait on those tables. There's only one in a hundred who will go out to knock on doors and ask those unreached people if they want Jesus.

Don't misunderstand me. Often Prima Donnas will work for Christ if you supply them with a nice room and gather a large crowd so that they can witness — but for them to go out on the highways and byways and compel the lost to come to Christ — the leafy saints are beyond that!

But Glory to God! God is not fooled by leaves. He proved that when he came to the fig tree. One must either produce or be withered and removed from the vineyard.

# Chapter 4

# Do Not Grow a Garden of Weeds

You have to keep weeds out of the garden. Weeds steal the moisture. Do you know what weeds are a sign of? Weeds are a sign of a lack of **dominion** over your environment.

My yard was eaten up with weeds. I had a bumper crop of weeds and I had to get rid of them. I was not responsible for all the weeds in the world, but only the weeds in my yard. There needs to be government in your yard. Get rough with the weeds. Tell them, "You weed! How dare you grow here! Get out!" There's a place for weeds and that place is **outside** the fence!

Likewise, inside the Kingdom of God the weeds rob the moisture from the earth. They choke the Word of God.

I have always liked to shake hands with everyone at the church. But now I'm beginning to understand why some preachers do not do this. I get attacked with all kinds of problems, problems, problems — weeds, weeds, weeds!

When I have come to exhort, I don't want a mouthful of weeds. I don't want weeds in my ears and weeds in my coat. I don't want to be weedy! I want to be seedy — every time I come to the pulpit.

Often I am attacked by Christians who have allowed weeds to grow in their gardens. These Christians have now become fruitless and want to act like something is wrong with the seed.

Friend, it is not the seed. Remember that the seed is the good Word of God. The problem is the wild growth of weeds in your garden. They're choking the plants — and causing them to become fruitless.

# YOU WERE NOT CREATED TO WORRY

In the Gospel according to Saint Mark, Jesus speaks of the cares of this world. Do you know what the cares of the world are? **Worry!**

Notice the voice of worry — "Oh, I don't know what I'm going to do. Income tax time is coming. The payment is due on the car. I'm worried to death!"

**Worry is a weed in your garden.** God has not created you to worry. He has not given you a spirit of fear. Fear to a man is like trying to run water through a diesel engine. It won't work!

I had an ulcer when I was 21 years old and was rather proud of it. At 21, I had already worried like a big shot. Worry is not one of the signs of a mature son of God.

If you go deer hunting, you look for deer droppings. I won't go into that too far, but there are rabbit droppings and there are deer droppings. At the end of the trail of rabbit droppings, don't expect to find a deer. However, at the end of the trail of deer droppings there will be a deer. If you are running around worrying you are not showing one of the signs of the Saint of God. The Saint of God doesn't leave a **trail of worry** everywhere he goes. Whatever the situation, the mature son of God knows he's safe with the Father!

Another weed God talks about in the scriptures is the deceitfulness of riches. There has been some beautiful teaching done across America about prosperity, but there is also something deceitful about it. When a man takes riches unto his own self, for his own benefit and to the exclusion of the benefit of the Kingdom of God, they will be of very little benefit to him. Riches will very quickly become weeds.

Don't misunderstand me. God **wants** you to be prosperous. The reason he wants you to be prosperous is so that you can walk 'The Love Walk'. This means that when you meet someone who has a need, you will be able to bless that person by meeting his need. God meant financial blessings to be part of the Christian life. Praise the Lord!

# Chapter 5

# The Treasures from the Good Ground

What do you find to be unique about good ground? Good ground is **controlled ground.** You have control of the birds. You make sure that everything is conducive to good root growth and you have control of the weeds. Now that you have the ground prepared, Jesus will come and He will give the increase!

This is why you find some pastors who live very godly lives, who serve the Lord, and who pastor only one hundred or so people. Praise God for that! This is not their decision. This is the Lord's decision. Remember — some thirty, some sixty, some a hundred. Always keep in mind that one plants, one waters, but **God gives the increase.** That is why there are some men who have ministries that reach hundreds of thousands of people. They have a controlled environment. They have weeded the garden. They've gotten rid of the 'birds' and the bad environment. They don't allow the weeds to grow. Such a person says, "Lord, I am ready to serve you. If you want me to pastor twenty people, I'm ready to do it. If you want me to pastor twenty thousand people, I'll pastor twenty thousand people. Lord, you set the pace for me. I'll plant, I'll water, but only you, Lord, can give the increase."

God can use a submissive man to reach tens of thousands — **millions** of people. Many will come to the Lord through such a man.

Listen to what the Bible says. "Are you not still babes?" Aren't you still just a little baby? That's what the scripture says. Are you on milk — little old milk-weed Christians? The Bible says, "Aren't you carnal?" Don't you realize that after the patch is weeded and

roots take hold, that God is the one who gives the increase. Never become confused on this point. **God gives the increases.**

When you see a small church where there is a faithful pastor who is preaching the Word of God and living the Life, you shouldn't go in with an arrogant attitude or with a critical spirit as to the size of that church. God is giving the increase — not that pastor. Good ground brings forth much fruit — some thirty, some sixty, some one hundred fold.

# Chapter 6

# What Is Your Secret, Brother John

Many people come to me and ask, "What's the secret of your ministry's success, Brother John?"

My secret is that I wake up excited. I wake up every morning 'drunk' on the Spirit of God and with anticipation of what God is doing for me and for the faithful in my congregation. I know pastors who are involved in many more activities than I am. I just read "The Book" and preach "The Word." People keep coming in, getting saved, and growing stronger and more fruitful — some thirty, some sixty, and some one hundred fold. I keep the 'birds' and 'weeds' under control, the root system in order, and God gives the increase.

Now take special notice, dear friend. If you will set your environment in order and walk forth from this time in the truth of God with the 'weeds' cleared from the garden, your root system deep in God's Word and the 'birds' gone, you may bring forth up to one hundred fold. However, if you bring forth only thirty fold, **that is a very good increase.**

"One plants and one waters, but God gives the increase." All we have to do is maintain the right environment, get rid of the 'birds' and 'weeds', and keep the roots strong. God promises the increase.

# Chapter 7

# The Spiritual Eye Sees

I wonder if you could get the picture of how your environment looks now. The Bible says, "Beware your adversary, like a roaring lion, walking about seeking whom he may devour." Within the spirit world, in your midst, **there is a lion walking about seeking to devour you!**

At this very moment, all around you, there are big 'buzzards' flying around. There are 'birds' waiting to steal your seeds. There are 'weeds' attempting to come up all around you. They want to confuse the issue, strangle your spiritual growth, and render you fruitless.

I am acutely aware of these 'birds'! They may be telling you that this message is really for the 'birds' . . . but I can see Satan's work — can you?

Jesus died for the sins of the world and He wants to save you. He wants to give you everlasting life, make you a new creature, remove you from the generation of Adam and put you into the Kingdom of His dear Son. He wants you to stop being a lost person and to start being a new creation in Christ Jesus. However, in spite of all this, the devil is sitting there like a 'bird'. He is waiting for the seed to hit your heart so he can devour it, foul the root system, or choke the growth with 'weeds' and make you fruitless.

Keep a **good** environment — one ready to bring forth a great thirty, sixty, hundred fold harvest to God, as **He** gives the increase.

My prayer is that God will bless you, in this endeavor.

# BOOK & TAPE
# CATALOGUE
# ON NEXT PAGES

# Order These Vital Books
# By
# Dr. Avanzini
# Today

*Over 500,000 copies are already sold!*

**Always Abounding**                                    **$5.00 U.S.A.**
This anointed book brings you into the daily, practical areas of giving and receiving, sowing and reaping — in a way that will seem like a whole new theology to many. But, every concept is founded on the Word. You must have this book!

**Stolen Property Returned!**                          **$6.00 U.S.A.**
This book has already changed thousands of lives! You have been ripped off by the most successful thief in the history of the universe — Satan. In this book, you will learn how to TAKE BACK WHAT SATAN HAS STOLEN. Learn how to regain your lost possessions, lost loved ones, lost reputation . . . literally anything that has been snatched from you by the devil. If you have ever lost anything to Satan, this book is a must for you.

**Financing the Endtime Harvest — God's Way**
**"Ninety Lessons and Twelve Summaries in the Principles of Biblical Economics"**                          **$7.00 U.S.A.**
God intends for His people to have "more than enough." To reap the final endtime harvest of souls, there must be major financial breakthroughs in the body of Christ.

Learn how you can BE A BLESSING TO others through these 90 powerful lessons on the Biblical Principles of Economics.

**The Wealth of the Wicked "Is Laid Up for the Just"**
                                                       **$7.00 U.S.A.**
This total Biblical revelation of the great endtime transfer of the wealth of the wicked rich into the hands of God's children is without a doubt the greatest revelation pertaining to finances in the church today. This book is a non-speculative Biblical documentary of the little known Bible teaching pertaining to the vast stockpile of wealth that the wicked systematically hoard, that God regularly takes from them and redistributes to His informed children. The book also proves from scripture that the time of the final and greatest transfer of this wealth has already started.

**Birds, Roots, Weeds, and The Good Ground**     **$2.50 U.S.A.**

Have you ever had the good seed of the gospel planted in your heart through a powerful message, only to forget it in hours? Well, this book teaches you how to stop the "birds, roots, and weeds" from destroying the "good ground" of the gospel seeds planted in your life.

**Paul's Thorn**     **$2.50 U.S.A.**

Once and for all, this book destroys the false concept that "sickness glorifies God." No longer can we settle for such perversions in God's word. God wants you well! This book shows how Paul never rejoiced in sickness, and never saw it as a chance to glorify God through pain. Buy several copies of this book and give them to those you know who are currently suffering with a sickness. It will bless them greatly!

## BROTHER JOHN'S POWERFUL TAPES ARE AVAILABLE TO YOU!

**1.** Seven Ways of Receiving Finances From God

**2.** Reaping in Your Recession

**3.** Receiving in Financial Trials

**4.** Why God Prospers His Children

**5.** More Than Enough

**6.** The Wealth of the Wicked Is Laid Up for the Just

Each tape individually is only $7.00 U.S.A. When you order, please specify both the number and title, and enclose your check payable to HIS IMAGE MINISTRIES.

On all orders, please add $1.00 for postage and handling. Thank you.

*ORDER ALL BOOKS OR TAPES FROM*
**HIS IMAGE MINISTRIES**
**BOX 1057**
**HURST, TEXAS U.S.A.**
**76053**

# NOTES

# NOTES

# NOTES